Take Charge of Your Success

Fight Like a Girl to Get What (and Where) You Want

Michele Sfaklanos, RN, BSN

ISBN 978-1-7322722-7-9

Printed in the United States of America

Because of the dynamic nature of the Internet, any Web addresses or links contained in this book may have changed since publication and may no longer be valid. The views expressed in this work are solely those of the author and do not necessarily reflect the views of the publisher, and the publisher hereby disclaims any responsibility for them.

Disclaimer

The information in this book is:

- of a general nature and not intended to address the specific circumstances of any particular individual or entity;
- written as a guide and is not intended to be a comprehensive tool, but is complete, accurate, or up to date at the time of writing;
- an information tool only and not intended to be used in place of a visit, consultation, or advice of a medical professional;

This book is not intended to serve as professional or legal advice (if you need specific advice, you should always consult a suitably qualified professional).

When it comes to fighting for what you want in your personal life or business, I believe everyone has the right to fight for what they want. They just need to know the proper steps to take to make it a good fight. This book is dedicated to your fight for the life you want!

Foreword

Before I jump into the introduction, I want to tell you something. I talk pretty openly about my faith in this book and will quote scripture from time to time. I do that because it has been an important part of my personal journey. It may also be a part of yours. But I also know that it may not be. Just know I will not try to force my faith on you. I sincerely believe you'll benefit from hearing this information.

In our society, to be told we "fight like a girl" implies weakness. Or, it's meant as an insult. But I ask you, have you ever seen a fight between two girls? There is a "no holds barred" type of commotion that goes on. Unlike men, it's not just punching that happens. Girls punch, pull hair, bite, pull at clothing and do everything they can to get the upper hand. They fight dirty. I've seen girl fights that put men fights to shame! That said it can be a scary thing to watch.

Girls are meant to fight like girls and not like men. Should they put themselves on a man's level and go toe-to-toe? Of course not, and I would never encourage that. When boys fight, they earn the respect of their peers. They are considered brave and strong when they fight for what is important to them. They are admired when they stand up for someone they care for, when they stand up to bullies, or to uphold their family name. When girls fight, their social status is challenged and most times they are just considered low-class. However, have you ever seen a mother protecting her young? Does she have the right to fight for her family? You better believe she does.

When it comes to fighting for what you want in your personal life or business, I believe everyone has the right to fight for what they want. They just need to know the proper steps to take to make it a good fight. Women were made to be tough. Look at what women go through with childbirth alone. Women endure pain, their body changes shape (and sometimes doesn't return to their original size), their hormones rage, and if that isn't enough, they have their beautiful baby and have to get up all hours of the night to care for the child, usually without any (or little) assistance from their partner. Let's face it, as much as women try to emerge in this world as something other than a wife or mother, there is still a lot of "old fashioned" mentality out there – you know – that the woman's place is still in the home.

As women, it's time to change this thinking for good. Let's learn to fight like a girl to get what (and where) we want!

Table of Contents

Authenticity

What does it mean to be authentic? Being authentic is the ability to be true to oneself. Living an authentic life requires the ability to be true to our own wants, needs and desires and not live our lives by the opinion of others. Being authentic is the ability to make self-honoring choices and stand firmly in who we are in our core. Authentic behavior is the subjective perception that one is behaving in a way that is in accordance with her core being. The sense of authenticity is considered an important component of the self.

The words "authentic" and "authenticity" are buzzwords that are thrown around in the media and in literature, but what does it really mean to live an authentic life?

In order to live an authentic type of life, we have to first know who we are. It requires that we stop looking outside ourselves for validation and appreciation and instead go inside and discover the true woman within us. When we connect to who we are at the core of our being, the light of truth engulfs us. It comes to us as a warm feeling of coming home and a charge of energy that explodes into every cell of our being. It is a feeling of connectedness to ourselves that can't be denied. Once we have truly connected with who we are, life as we know it is forever transformed. A new confidence and a new awareness take us places we may have never imagined possible.

When we stay connected to our true self at the center of our being, we live our lives in pure authenticity. We love who we are and no longer feel the need or desire to live by the expectations of anyone outside ourselves. We are able to listen to ourselves and know what is best for us. We know what brings us the greatest joy and fulfillment and we no longer allow guilt to prevent us from being who we need to be.

Being true to ourselves gives us the insight and compassion to see others, for who they are, not who we expect them to be. It frees us up from the judgment of ourselves and others and it gives others the freedom to be themselves as well. When we are true to the woman within us, our authenticity and integrity spills out into our world and allows us to live our lives in unconditional love and acceptance.

But we find that women aren't always true to themselves. In a vain attempt to live up to business norms and societal expectations, their behaviors sometimes go against their own values. I remember as a young divorced mother of two, when I started out in the business world, I did everything I could to please others and to always do a good job. I didn't realize the toll it was taking on my two children. I would work late hours leaving them with a babysitter and when I picked them up and came home, it felt like we rushed through dinner, bath and bedtime. I didn't spend quality time with them that they deserved. It wasn't long before I realized being a phony isn't easy. I found that it takes a lot of energy to behave in ways that were out of sync with my true values, priorities, hopes, characteristics, and style. The energy spent trying to come across as something you are not is energy unavailable for work, other activities, and, most of all, your family.

The alternative to this predicament is authenticity— a healthy alignment between your values and behaviors that can reenergize life at work and at home. When I finally discovered this balance, life became so much better for me and my children.

Women who are authentic have a good understanding of themselves and their priorities. They attend first to what is important to them rather than what might be important to other people. They are clear about how they feel and what they need and prefer.

Authenticity is best thought of as a condition or dynamic balance—and not a personality trait. As a goal, it is not clearly defined like earning a college degree. And, achieving authenticity doesn't mean it's yours to keep. You have to work to remain authentic. You have to review your priorities and choose behaviors that match those priorities as circumstances change. It is difficult to develop your capabilities when you are suppressing your true values and style or are distracted by inner conflict. But living a life strongly connected to your belief system promotes growth, learning, and psychological well-being. That makes authenticity an important factor in your personal development.

So, what can individuals do to develop authenticity? How can we align our inner and outer selves so our behavior becomes comfortable and natural, allowing us to be better people?

There are specific steps each of us can take to better align our inner and outer selves. But know that the process of becoming an authentic person isn't easy. It doesn't happen all at once, and it certainly doesn't happen overnight. You have to work to become and remain authentic, reviewing your priorities and choosing behaviors that reflect those priorities as your circumstances change. It requires continuous effort and overcoming hurdles–from societal norms to business cultures - but the rewards can be great for all involved.

Here are some steps to get you started:

Step One: Increase Your Self-Awareness - A key component of behaving authentically is to understand what you care about most. What are your values, your likes, and your dislikes? This might sound simple, but in today's complex world filled with a wide variety of choices, pressures, and distractions, selecting what is most important to us can be difficult.

Step Two: Assess and Evaluate - Once you've established your priorities and values, and likes and dislikes, you can better understand how aligned your behaviors are with your values. You may need to review what you have already given up—and what you are willing to give up to get what is most important to you. Ask yourself what you need to let go of to better align your behaviors with your beliefs. Maybe it's time to delegate some of your job duties so you can take on new responsibilities. You might need to sacrifice leisure activities so you can make the most of a career opportunity, or accept slower progress up the management ladder to spend more time with your family. Or, you might want to build a nonprofit that addressees a social problem that is important to you.

There are no "right" trade-offs to make, and your choices will likely change at various points in your life. The crucial thing is to be clear on what is most important to you now, and what you will and will not do to get there. Know what really motivates you. This clarity will position you to establish authenticity.

Step Three: Take Action - This is where the going gets really tough. It's one thing to be aware of your priorities and decide which trade-offs you are willing to make, but it is quite another to make real changes in your life. You don't need to make big changes all at once. You can start with small steps and gradually align your behaviors with your most important values. If, for example, the most important thing to you is to improve the relationships in your personal life, you might cut back on the number of weekend hours you spend in the office or on business travel, so you can be with family and friends. Although at first you might feel your decreased time at work will hurt your job performance, your increased sense of well-being will make you a more productive person and a better leader.

Step Four: Get Support - In any area of personal development, getting support from other people can help you achieve your goals. If you share your goals about authenticity with those you love and trust, you will create a source of feedback and reinforcement that can make it easier to stay on track. At the same time, it's important to believe in yourself and the legitimacy of your values. Trust your instincts. Please – trust your instincts. Just know there will be times when acting authentically requires going against what your boss, colleagues, family members, or friends advise you to do – and that's okay.

Developing authenticity often requires taking risks. Have faith in your own judgment about what is right for you. Regardless of our status in the corporate world, or the community, a woman is to be authentic to herself and others in order to be taken seriously.

Authenticity

NOTES

Beauty and Integrity

It's not your imagination: Life is good for beautiful people. Research over the past decades has found that attractive people earn more than their average-looking peers, are more likely to be given loans by banks, and are less likely to be convicted by a jury. Voters prefer better-looking candidates; students prefer better-looking professors, while teachers prefer better-looking students. Mothers, those icons of blind love, have been shown to favor their more attractive children.

Perhaps even more discouraging, we tend to assume that beautiful people are actually better people—in realms that have nothing to do with physical beauty. Study after study has shown that we judge attractive people to be healthier, friendlier, more intelligent, and more competent than the rest of us, and we use even the smallest differences in attractiveness to make these judgments. A startling study published earlier this year found that even identical twins judge each other by relative beauty: The more attractive twin assessed the other as less athletic, less emotionally stable, and less socially competent. The less attractive twins agreed, ranking their better-looking siblings ahead of them.

Still, the issue has generated few serious solutions. Though to a surprising degree, we agree on who is attractive and who isn't. Differences in looks remain largely unmentionable, unlike divisions of race, gender, disability, or sexual orientation. How do you change a discriminatory behavior that, even though unfair, is obviously deep, hard to pin down, and largely unconscious—and affects people who would be hurt even to admit they're in this type of category?

Many businesses are now using technology to help fight the issue. The field of industrial psychology has developed a set of best practices for businesses that want to avoid discrimination in hiring, including the use of online or standardized interviews that remove an interviewer's unreliable gut instincts from the equation. Other best practices include scoring interview answers numerically, and committing to ask every candidate the exact same set of questions, since subtle bias often appears in the form of extra follow-up questions.

This is why I love the show "The Voice." The judges have their backs to the performers. They only hear the voices of those singing and are not able to see them until they have turned their chair around to try and get them on their team.

Our preference for beautiful people makes us poor judges of qualities that have nothing to do with physical appearance—it means that when we select employees, teachers, protégés, borrowers, and even friends, we may not really be making the best choice. It's an embarrassing and stubborn truth—and the question is now whether social researchers can find a way to help us level the playing field.

Beauty, as it turns out, is not in the eye of the beholder. Generally, it means feminine features for women, like large eyes and a round face, and masculine features for men, like a square jaw. Even newborn infants have been shown to prefer gazing at faces adults agree are attractive.

The Constitution forbids employment discrimination on the basis of things like race, sex, and religion, but only a few jurisdictions have tried to add appearance to the list, starting with the parts of appearance you can measure.

It's clear that we trust beauty beyond the realms in which it actually makes a difference. Beautiful people may be likelier to receive loans and receive lower interest rates, but research says they're just as likely to default. That alone suggests there are areas where more objective kinds of evaluation would be helpful.

One means of attack is perhaps the simplest of all: There's a chance that merely making us aware of the bias can help diffuse it, by allowing us to remind ourselves that we're wrong if we assume that beautiful and good are one and the same. Prolonged exposure to media images distorts our brain's notion of that "average" face. In a plugged-in era in which I see Jennifer Aniston's face more than my own sister's, my brain's concept of "average" is distorted wildly far from reality. It's up to us to put down the beauty magazines and take a stance.

You are probably wondering by this point why I included Integrity with Beauty in this chapter. I want you to realize that beauty IS skin deep and we need to look beyond the beauty to see the person inside. That's what really matters. Does that beautiful person live with integrity?

Carl Jung said: "Your vision will become clear only when you look into your heart. Who looks outside, dreams. Who looks inside, awakens."

When we are fortunate enough to experience those moments in life where things come together, when through our own actions we seize the day and utilize golden opportunities, we are able to create lasting changes in life and realize goals. Leading our lives with integrity means that we are living to our fullest potential and are able to create and manifest our destinies. When we are truly aligned with our life purpose, it is easy to stay committed to our goals and dreams and feel fulfillment on a daily basis, no matter what we look like.

Being truly aligned is something that has to be practiced regularly. Life has a wonderful habit of providing us with variety. Just as emotions and experiences are fleeting, so is integrity. Falling out of sync with your life is what happens regularly if you aren't living life to its fullest.

Here are 5 Tips for a Life of Integrity.

1. Appreciate the speed bumps. Of course, it sucks to have to slow down and acknowledge that we are not where we want to be, or things aren't moving along as planned. It is especially

hard if you realize that your detour is self-inflicted, but it is important to notice the power in this awareness.

When a plane is flying to a destination, it is never flying in a straight path. In fact, the pilot and all of the fancy computers on board are constantly recalculating and realigning their direction to ensure that they are on track. That is the beauty of any journey. Be aware that it takes consistent awareness and continual realignment to ensure that we are on track with where we want to go in life.

If you're not comfortable in your life by not living in full integrity with what you want for yourself, consider that feeling as a beacon to get you where you really want to go. Use this experience as a gift to check in regularly and hone in on what needs to be revised in your life.

2. Know your outcome. It is impossible to not experience distress and internal turmoil when you feel aimless in life. It is also impossible not to feel aimless in life if you have no idea where you want to go.

Take the time to figure out what it is that you really want. This requires some soul searching, asking tough questions and maybe even experiencing some painful emotions that come up when we are faced with not living with integrity. Map out your life and what you want it to look like. Create the most outrageously amazing vision for your life if you could have it all. Once you find out what makes you passionate about life, you can figure out what you need to do to get there, and perhaps realize what is preventing you from getting there at all.

The most important step to living a life with integrity is realizing that you have to live true to what you alone really want, and realize whether your daily actions, your job or career path, and your relationships are true to you.

3. Anchor yourself. One of the best tools I use in my daily life is an anchor for integrity. To me, integrity is a strong word that evokes a lot of feelings and passion for my life and where I want it to go. A strong word can be anchor enough for some to really engage in their lives and live fully to their highest standards. For those who need something more, a physical anchor can be a powerful tool too.

An anchor can be anything from a rock, a button, a piece of jewelry, to a page of your journal stored in your wallet for easy access. Some people like to reread reminders of their goals and dreams, while others prefer a more physical approach by rubbing a favorite stone.

I personally enjoy the use of gem stones for anchors in my life. I like to look at what qualities certain gem stones are traditionally associated with. I find myself more aligned to those qualities when I rub the stones. An anchor is anything you use to ground yourself, a regular reminder of who you truly are and all you are working toward that you can always access.

4. Gratitude & Giving Back. I believe in the importance of practicing daily gratitude as a rule. In living a life of integrity, gratitude can help you stay focused on what you really want and keep you present in your goals and dreams. I believe that you can never feel too blessed about where you are in your life. Only good things come from taking the time to flood your heart with positive emotion and gratitude. The ripple effect of daily gratitude can be clearly felt in your life if you're consistent.

To enhance your gratitude experience, consider giving back to a cause you believe in. Oftentimes we wait for the holidays to roll around, when we are often too busy or our purse strings too tight to give back to those in need. People traditionally experience guilt at times in life where we should be most passionate about celebrating our blessings. I invite you to consider giving back not because you should, but because you can. Do it now. Find a cause that speaks to you, such as a cancer society, a youth-at-risk shelter or perhaps even a museum. Consider giving just a few hours, one day a month, to do something to help out - just because. Volunteering for a cause you believe in is such a wonderful experience, and really puts so much of our lives into perspective. A life of integrity starts with our actions from the heart.

5. State your intentions. If you know who you are and what you want, don't wait to live your life. Nothing will change in your life if you are able to soul search, discover your passions, and then not decide that something needs to change. Even if you are

15

rediscovering your purpose, or just restating what you are already working towards, say it out loud.

Integrity comes from within. Have courage to be the author, editor and illustrator for your own epic life. Beauty is what is on the inside, but it never hurts to add a little sparkle to the outside!

NOTES

Clarity

Clarity is that strong and unwavering sense that our daily choices are grounded in an authentic sense of purpose. Clarity is how we create a sketch of something worth asking others to complete. Clarity forces us to form the right questions.

Without clarity everything we do is an attempt to gain the hope that we are moving in the right direction.

Clarity does not emerge by simply switching on some beacon in hopes of throwing a clear and guiding light. No, it comes when we discover a rusted but sturdy lamp in the antique store. Then, only through careful tinkering and polishing this lamp begins to cast a flicker of light. And, as we continue to polish and tinker, something truly brilliant begins to evolve.

With clarity comes control. With clarity comes grace. With clarity comes joy.

Finding and keeping clarity takes work. It takes an unbending willingness to see things for what they really are. To be able to filter decisions based on what might be best for ourselves and others.

Clarity is both a feeling and a direction. It can be experienced and seen. It is at the same time perfect simplicity and obvious complexity. Clarity inspires us and those around us.

But what is it exactly?
- Clarity is doing more with less
- Clarity is embracing the truth
- Clarity is anticipating needs
- Clarity is measuring one perfect thing
- Clarity is forming decisions out of beliefs

Clarity is the most important idea in both business and your personal goals; therefore, lack of clarity is probably more responsible for frustration and underachievement than any other single factor. That's why we say that "Success is goals and all else is commentary." People with clear, written goals, accomplish far more in a shorter period of time than people without them could ever imagine. This is true everywhere and under all circumstances.

Our vision comes first. If you have a clear vision of what you want, you will eventually attract the right strategy to get it. If you clearly see your wants and desires, you greatly increase the odds that one day you will live it.

In order to gain clarity and have a clear picture, focus on what you want. You might have a blurry picture at first, but in order to achieve what you want, bring that picture into clear focus. You don't have to have every little detail thought out before you move forward. The big idea needs to be clear and the rest will become clear as you move forward. You will need to make adjustments along the way – it's a part of life.

If your journey is worth taking, it is worth defining. Bringing clarity can be difficult and time consuming. You simply can't reach an uncertain destination.

Napoleon Hill said: "There is one quality that one must possess to win, and that is definiteness of purpose, the knowledge of what one wants, and a burning desire to possess it."

Clarity of purpose is vital for the achievement of success and for making dreams come true. Your dream or goal must be specific and clear, and not vague. While it's fun to daydream about being rich and successful, you have to know and define clearly what you want to get or to achieve.

Clarity of purpose is important for every kind of success, whether it's losing weight, getting a new car or traveling abroad. If you don't know exactly what you want, how can you get it? When there is clarity of purpose you know what steps to take.

With clarity of purpose you focus on the goal, without wasting time or energy. Clarity of purpose is like focusing a strong source of light on your goal, so that you see it clearly.

The 10 steps to attain clarity of purpose are:

1. Know what you want. What gives us joy, evokes our passion, makes time stop?
2. Investigate why you want to achieve your goal, and what you will gain by achieving it.
3. Be certain that you really want to achieve your goal, and you aren't doing it for someone else.
4. Read and learn about your goal.
5. Seek out pictures about your goal.
6. Visualize your goal clearly. In your mind, see all the details. Be specific as to color, size, quantity, shape, place, smells, sounds, etc., of what you want to get or accomplish.
7. Time to write it down, clearly and in detail.
8. Learn to focus your mind on your goal.
9. Remove clutter from your life. Remove the self-doubt and the naysayers from your life.
10. Display perseverance and some self-discipline in your life.

Fewer than three percent of adults have written goals and plans that they work on every single day. When you sit down and write out your goals, you move yourself into the top 3% of people in our society. And you will soon start to get the same results they do.

When I first started writing my goals, I would write a short-term goal first. I started easy at first to build my confidence in my abilities. Then I worked up to larger goals. I like to take long-term goals and break them into smaller goals in order to keep things simple and to be able to clearly define what I am after. In setting my goals, I make sure to set deadlines that are manageable, especially with a busy schedule. I found that if I set the deadlines too tight, I was more willing to give up along the way.

Once you have set your goals, study and review them every day to be sure they are still your top priorities. You will find yourself adding goals to your list as time passes. You will also find yourself deleting goals that are no longer as important as you once thought. Whatever your goals are, plan them out thoroughly, on paper, and work on them every single day. This is the key to peak performance and maximum achievement.

How aware are you of your life's clarity and purpose, you know - your soul's calling?

To help you answer that - ask yourself the following questions:

- What have been your most enjoyable achievements in life so far?
- If you could do, be or have anything you wanted, what would you choose?
- What would you do if you knew you could not fail?
- You are given a billion dollars. What do you do?
- Who inspires you? What qualities do they have you most admire?

Once you have the answers to these questions, here is your action to take:

First, make a list of 5-10 goals that you would like to achieve in the coming year. Write them down in the present tense, as though a year has passed and you have already accomplished them. For example, "I am" or "I have" – not "I want" or "I wish."

Second, from your list of these goals, ask yourself, "What one goal, if I were to accomplish it, would have the greatest "positive" impact on my life?" Whatever it is, put a circle around this goal and move it to a separate sheet of paper. Make this goal your major purpose for the weeks and months ahead.

Third, set a deadline, make a plan, and put it into action and work on it every day. Make sure that for each item on your list, you set a time and date when you will take action.

The last step is to wash, rinse, and repeat – wash, rinse, and repeat and get ready for some amazing changes in your life.

Immerse yourself in activities that you enjoy doing or think you might like doing. Sometimes we don't even attempt things that we may want to do because of a lack of time, money or talent. The reality is that there are things that you can do now without waiting for more time in your day or a huge lottery win.

Want to set up a charitable foundation? Start small. Begin by giving more of yourself. Think generously about others. Donate old clothes and household items to a thrift shop. Donate your time by volunteering at the local soup kitchen. Take small steps in the right direction. Small steps are better than sitting still. Just take action.

Getting clear about what you do want is a process of trial and error. Try something. Ask yourself - Do I like this? Yes. No. The key is to do more of what you enjoy and you will continually clarify what it is that you want to do, be, and have in your life. This is why defining your clarity of purpose is so important.

Your clarity of purpose provides both a foundation and launching pad for your personal and professional success. The old saying, "If you don't know where you're going, you won't know when you get there" is a cliché but true. Getting clear on your personal definition of success is the first step.

If you haven't already done so, I suggest you take some time and think about your clarity of purpose. How do you define personal and professional success for yourself? Keep that purpose and definition of success in mind as you go about your daily business.

The common sense point here is simple. Defining your personal clarity of purpose is the first step in being a personal and professional success. Use your purpose in life to guide your career and life decision making. Once you are clear on what you want from life, it becomes relatively easy to determine what you need to do to get you there. It all begins with clarity – and only you can determine what success means for you.

NOTES

Faith

Most us probably fear things that we shouldn't really fear—like a routine dentist appointment or that teeny tiny crawling spider—and even though we realize, rationally, that we shouldn't fear something so silly, we just can't seem to help it. Most of the time these little fears don't hinder us too much, but there are times when they can prevent us from making positive choices. There are times when they can prevent us from living in the present—like when you spend time outside searching for that potential bug encounter.

Are you frustrated because you know you're not doing what you are meant to do? Are you letting fear rule you? Learning to fight with faith is the answer.

I wonder how many people actually have gifts and talents from God, but they aren't using them because they tried once and failed?

So many people are frustrated because they know they're not doing what they are meant to do and are letting fear rule them.

I want you to get an "ah – ha moment" or revelation about this because you're not going to ever be really happy if you don't fulfill your potential and be who God created you to be. The key is to learn who you are in Christ and see yourself in Him.

So whatever Jesus is, we are too. He is strong, and in Him, we are strong. He is courageous; in Him, we are courageous. He is a conqueror, so we can be too. He has peace and joy, so we have peace and joy. He's capable and bold. In Christ, we can do whatever we need to do with His boldness.

Everyone experiences fear in their life. There are big fears we are very aware of and little ones we may not even realize we have.

I've learned that it's very important to understand what fear is and how it works against us. If we don't recognize our fears, it can keep us from becoming what God created us to be, which means we won't fulfill our purpose in life.

Mind-crippling, spine-tingling, heart-stomping fear – we've all experienced it at one time or another. We're not talking about the good kind of fear that alerts your spirit to an approaching enemy, that moves you into action to protect the ones you love, or that promotes a healthy respect for God. Those fears are healthy. And not all fears are irrational. Some move in and out quickly without disrupting our lives.

But what about the other kind? Where does irrational fear originate? And how do you keep those fears from taking perma- nent residence in your life?

The problem with such thoughts is that they bring with them unwarranted anxiety and stress. If you would rather not experience the emotional fallout due to irrationality, here are 10 ways to arrest this kind of thinking.

1. Address your emotional responses. The first key to dealing with any fear is admitting to it (not always easy if, say, the fear is a bug and you are an adult!). And the next key thing is to recognize your emotional and/or physical—heart beating fast, muscles tensing up, palms sweating, and responses to the fear. Sometimes fear—especially the irrational kind—can take over and we don't even realize how afraid we are of something until we start paying attention to our own signals. When we pay attention to how we are feeling and when we are feeling that way, we are able to work with those emotional responses rather than simply react to them.

2. Consider negativity as a red flag. Irrationality is often characterized by negativity. Perhaps the idea came from your own insecurity or it could have been an insinuation from another person that you somehow internalized. But whenever you put forth an idea that somehow brings you down, stop. Take a step back. Ask yourself: What is the basis of this idea that I have? Am I being paranoid? Am I blowing this incident way out of proportion? Am I being inflexible? More importantly, if I continue with this line of thoughts, is it in any way conducive to personal growth? Am I not hurting myself with this kind of thinking?

3. Turn negativity into affirmation. Decide not to passively accept defeat and irrational thinking. Ask yourself: "So what? Even if it were true, does it necessarily mean that I am powerless to change it?" Restructure your thinking in such a way as to encourage positive change: "I will rise above this. I will not put myself down. I believe I am a good person and I deserve to be happy." "I have no fear."

4. Meditate and be mindful of your strengths and weaknesses. Meditation is one way of keeping yourself grounded, and keeping your thoughts in line. It can be partly introspection, partly therapy. You can discipline your mind to be calm as you sort out these thoughts, removing the ideas that cause the worst damage. Face your fears from a safe headspace.

5. Ask for advice. You are not alone. Do not be embarrassed to ask for advice. You may also compare your version of reality with that of other people, particularly those people close to you whom you can count on to tell you the truth. This is not about letting other people think for you – it's about looking at all sides of the equation. So, you have a theory. Test your theory. Gather more data. Compare or contrast. Alter your version so that it encompasses more than just your narrow viewpoint. This is also a way of gaining perspective.

6. Use your senses to stay present. While I'm anticipating the worse, I'm missing out on what's actually happening in the present—what I can see, smell, taste, touch, and hear. Instead of directing my attention to what I'm going to be afraid of in the

future, it's best for me to focus on what's happening now, which includes all of the beautiful things around me. Rather than worry about what's coming, we need to redirect our attention to what's here.

7. Get (gradual) exposure to what you fear. It can be hard to actually expose yourself to what you're afraid of (just looking at photos of spiders online sends shivers of disgust down my spine), but when the fear must be conquered, it's key to start gradually coming to terms with the fear. I've started doing this by looking at them online, and, while I won't say it's really helped that much yet, I have a feeling I'll be less surprised when I en-counter one of these guys in real life.

8. Recall what you've conquered. I've been through many different fearful circumstances in my life and each and every time I've made it through; I've conquered this same scenario many times. Even when I recall the unpleasant experiences I've had, I realize that, in the big picture, most things don't really impact my life that much. The irrational fear is just that—irra-tional—and by revisiting the situations you've already been through; you will feel stronger and better prepared to take on your fear.

9. Take it one day at a time. Instead of worrying about the unpleasant things coming, focus on today. The unpleasant hasn't arrived. And when it does, focus on that day and that moment instead of worrying about whether or not your fear will take over. To cope with any irrational fear, it can be so helpful to take it

one day, hour, or minute at a time. Instead of worrying about the future—the trick is to focus on getting through little bits of time. It's much easier to master a fear when you tell yourself you only have to do it for a short period of time. And all those short periods of time add up.

10. Be kind to yourself. You are not the first person to think or behave irrationally. You will not be the last. People do it all the time. The point is not that you have irrational thoughts, but what you do to minimize their impact on you. Maybe, just maybe, your overthinking is just a signal to take better care of yourself. Are you eating or sleeping right? Are you managing your habits? Are you stressed at work and haven't had a vacation in a while? Take a day off and pamper yourself a little. You do not have to be strong all of the time. You do not always have to have your ducks in a row. Give yourself a break.

Recognize that irrational fear does not originate with God. For God has not given us a spirit of fear, but of power and of love and of a sound mind (1 Timothy 1:7).

Fear is a tool the devil uses against us to make us miserable and destroy our lives. It begins as a thought and then creates emotions that can rule us. It often becomes a strong, intense feeling that tries to move us to make a foolish action or tries to prevent us from doing something that would be good for us. Because it's such a common way that Satan attacks people's lives, I think of it as the master spirit he uses to manipulate people and keep them out of God's will.

Simply put, fear is the opposite of faith. God wants us to walk by faith, and Satan wants us to walk by fear. When we learn to live by faith and not let fear rule our life, we can live a fulfilling, satisfying, peaceful and joyful life.

Listen to these words and adapt them as your own:

As I begin each new day, I step out in faith. I am excited to know that God has given me all I need to have a great life. The energy, life, and love of Spirit move through me easily and effortlessly. I open to divine ideas and discern what is mine to do. I am blessed with unlimited possibilities to experience life. I feel one with all that is. I feel certain that my circumstances will work out favorably, perhaps in unimaginable ways. I am meant to live a great life!

NOTES

Influence

Influence - the capacity to have an effect on the character, development, or behavior of someone or something, or the effect itself.

The world is constantly moving. Data is swirling around in all directions. And at times, you may feel like you're at the center of it all. So many things can influence you, such as a familiar sweet smell at a bakery, a picture hanging on a wall, or even just a color on a piece of clothing.

I'm going to talk about nine sources of influence that are affecting you every day. These sources are at the heart of your day to-day choices, and have a far-reaching effect on how you live your life as well as whether you're satisfied or frustrated with your life, overall.

1. Self-talk. That which goes through your mind when making a decision is often subtle and easy to miss, but often powerful. The things you say to yourself in your head can empower you or make you feel completely powerless. They can cause you to pause and think about your next action, or drive you to make choices mindlessly.

2. Previous Experiences. If your current circumstances resemble experiences you've had before, that may push you to

make the same familiar choice you made before...or compel you to make a different one. Even experiences we've long forgotten can influence our choices years later.

3. Environment. When you're in unfamiliar surroundings, you may feel uptight or vulnerable; your confidence might be low which can cause you to make conservative decisions when the opposite might be best. If you're in a familiar environment, you may feel at ease or empowered, which will influence your choices in a different direction. However, if you're in a familiar environment where good or bad things may have happened, again, that will influence your emotional state, your thoughts, and your actions.

4. Senses. What you're seeing, touching, tasting, or smelling can influence how you perceive your environment and how you feel, emotionally. Sensory feedback is hitting you constantly and can cause you to feel as you did in past experiences, both good and bad, without you knowing why you feel the way you do.

5. People. Whether through peer pressure, or a fondness toward someone, just being with other people can cause you to eliminate some choices as options and make other choices much more likely for you to choose.

6. The Future. When faced with a decision, in an instant, you will have considered the potential outcomes of many choices. If you want to avoid a specific outcome or effect, you'll make a choice that you believe will avoid it. If you desire a specific

outcome, you'll make a choice that you think will bring that potential future.

7. Media. Things read on the Internet, heard on the news or from a friend, or perhaps read in a textbook or magazine, can influence your choices. Sometimes what you hear in a song or on the radio can affect you, and the information doesn't even have to be accurate.

8. Your Physical Health. When you're feeling sick, tired, weak, clogged up, dried out, fried out, or inside out, you may not be at your best when making some choices. You could be so focused on how you feel that you don't thoroughly consider all your options and instead make the choices that require the least number of brain cells to make.

9. Your Mental Health. This includes your general emotional state, overall, but also specific states like depression, anger, etc. If you're feeling depressed, stressed out, anxious or cloudy-headed, making rational decisions isn't likely to be your first concern. Things you may normally care about take a back seat until you get past your funk. If the situation you find yourself in causes familiar and habitual emotions to stir, whether good or bad, your emotional state can directly affect your behavior and the choices you end up making.

You're constantly being influenced by what goes on in your head and what's happening around you. Being more aware of how you are influenced can help you think and make decisions more rationally. Consider the effects of your choices by first looking at the causes or influences around you. Just being more aware of these sources of influence can help you begin to slowly change what you don't like about your life or begin to mindfully enjoy what you do like about it.

Influence is, simply put, the power and ability to personally affect others' actions, decisions, opinions or thinking. At one level, it is about compliance, about getting someone to go along with what you want them to do. But you often need genuine commitment from others to accomplish key goals and tasks.

True commitment means you have succeeded in influencing people so that they'll endorse and truly support you or your task or plan. And in today's turbulent economy, when you're implementing big change, cutting back on resources or dealing with tough challenges, get all the commitment or engagement, you can.

When you influence people so they reach a place of genuine commitment, working relationships begin to improve. You see greater sustained effort and resiliency. Your colleagues become more efficient, creative and focused.

There are three kinds of influencing tactics: logical, emotional and cooperative. We call them influencing with head, heart and hands.

A logical appeal taps into people's reason and intellect. You present an argument for the best choice of action based on organizational benefits, personal benefits or both.

Most of us know how to talk about the organizational benefits of our ideas or plans. We explain the reasons for our proposed actions objectively and logically, with factual and detailed evidence for their feasibility and importance. We explain clearly and logically why these actions are the best possible. When challenged, we explain how potential organizational problems or concerns can be handled.

Less routine, but still common, is the personal logical appeal, explaining how a requested action is likely to benefit a person's career long term. You can take it a step further by helping the person gain more visibility and a better reputation within the organization, or by making a job easier or more interesting.

An emotional appeal connects your message, goal or project to individual goals and values. Link your request to a clear and appealing vision the other person can fully support. Describe the task with enthusiasm, and express confidence in the person's ability to accomplish it.

Of course, to make an emotional appeal you want some type of relationship with an understanding of the person you're appealing to. A misguided or uninformed emotional appeal can backfire. Generally, an idea that promotes a person's sense of well-being, service or belonging has the best chance of gaining support.

A cooperative appeal builds a connection between you, the person you want to influence and others, to get support for your proposal. Working together to accomplish a mutually important goal means you're extending a hand to others in the organization. It is an extremely effective way of influencing. Building cooperative connections may involve collaboration (figuring out what you will do together), consultation (finding out what ideas other people have), and alliances (drawing on whoever already supports you).

The most effective influencers know how to utilize all three approaches: logic, emotion and cooperation. To maximize your personal influence, you'll want to evaluate your own style of influencing. What tactics do you use most? What could you do differently? For example, if you rely exclusively on logical appeals, you'll miss the chance to engage people through their emotions, values and relationships. If you overemphasize emotional or cooperative appeals, you may leave out the data and rationales that will make your case.

Once you are more aware of your influencing style, you'll be able to become a more versatile—and more effective—leader.

I found six universal principles of influence—those that are so powerful that they generate desirable change in the widest range of circumstances. The principles are:

Influence

1. Reciprocation. People are significantly more willing to comply with requests (for favors, services, information, concessions, etc.) from a leader who has provided such things first.
2. Commitment/Consistency. People are more willing to be moved by a leader if they see the change as consistent with commitments they have previously and publicly made.
3. Authority. The particular combination of expertise and trustworthiness renders a leader the most persuasive communicator science has ever uncovered.
4. Social Validation. People are more willing to perform a recommended action if a leader provides evidence that many similar others are performing it.
5. Scarcity. People find recommended opportunities more attractive to the degree that a leader can honestly position them as scarce, rare, or dwindling in availability.
6. Liking. People say yes to the leaders they like. It's that simple – people say yes to leaders they like.

I also found nine ways to make people like you from Dale Carnegie. If you haven't read Dale Carnegie's books – I highly recommend them:

- Don't criticize, condemn, or complain.
- Give honest and sincere appreciation.
- Arouse in the other person an eager want.
- Become genuinely interested in other people.

- Smile
- Remember that a person's name is to that person the sweetest and most important sound in any language.
- Be a good listener. Encourage others to talk about themselves.
- Talk in terms of the other person's interests.
- Make the other people feel important – and do it sincerely.

There are 6 ways to influence others and win people to our way of thinking.

1. The only way to get the best of an argument is to avoid it.
2. Show respect for the other person's opinions. Never say, "You're wrong."
3. If you are wrong, admit it quickly and emphatically.
4. Begin in a friendly way.
5. Get the other person saying "yes, yes" immediately.
6. Let the other person do a great deal of the talking.

Lastly, if you want to influence people to follow you as a leader, be willing to do the job of a leader. A leader's job often includes changing your people's attitudes and behavior. Some suggestions to accomplish this:

- Begin with praise and honest appreciation.
- Call attention to people's mistakes indirectly.

- Talk about your own mistakes before criticizing the other person.
- Ask questions instead of giving direct orders.
- Let the other person save face.
- Praise the slightest improvement and praise every improvement. Be "hearty in your approbation and lavish in your praise."
- Give the other person a fine reputation to live up to.
- Use encouragement. Make the fault seem easy to correct.
- Make the other person happy about doing the thing you suggest.

Be the influence you want to see in others.

NOTES

Passion

We've heard it over and over that we need to have passion in order to start living with intention; that meaningful lives can be created through following one's passion.

Yet, while true to some extent, it's also a myth, because passion alone is simply not enough.

Rather, there needs to be a delicate balance of passion, but conviction as well. Being passionate about something is great, but it's rendered meaningless unless we have the courage–the conviction–to actually do something with it.

So just what is passion? Where does passion come from? Passion is a strong feeling of enthusiasm or excitement for something or about doing something. It's an enthusiasm that not only gives you energy and focus in the present, but also gives you power to keep moving toward the future. It gives you fuel to energize your journey.

Passion is a critical element for anyone who wants to achieve anything of significance in life. Passion is the starting point of all achievement. It is the energy of passion that makes things happen. Having passion is a choice.

The road to achievement is cluttered with detours, problems, and some disappointments. Many people can't get past the signs and problems and they never get to their destination. That's why passion is so important.

It is our passion that fuels us to face adversity. It carries us through the toughest of times. Passion gives you the energy to believe, plan, decide, prepare, begin and persist on our journey.

Too many people in the world are living lives of quiet desperation. They get up, go to a job they don't like, come home and watch a few hours of TV, go to bed, and do it all over again the next day. That's not a life.

Some of us have lives less desperate than this, but still we feel empty and unhappy. Maybe we have times of happiness and fun, but mostly we think about the life we wish we were living. Even though we don't quite know what that would look like.

When I talk about finding and living your life passion, I mean far more than finding a career you love or a hobby that's entertaining or volunteer work that is fulfilling. I'm talking about an entire lifestyle that is soaked with passion and powered by a passion source. That passion source may manifest in a career or avocation or something else entirely. But whatever it is, it colors the entirety of your life for the better.

When I talk about life passion, I'm talking about something big. Something bold. A total mind shift that changes the way you think about yourself and how you operate in the world.

Does that mean you have to give up your job or start over? Not necessarily. But maybe. It depends on you and what is most important, and less important, and worth sacrificing or pursuing based on your particular desires for a passionate life. Are you confused?

Let's make it simple. Decide you want a passionate life because you believe it's a goal worth pursuing. Once you decide to pursue it, the details are manageable.

But most people don't get that far. They don't get past the first gate when they think about life passion and allow their minds to wander a bit toward what it might take them to get there. Then they turn around and scurry back to the status quo.

They don't see passion as a goal worth pursuing because they aren't clear on the result. They don't know what a passionate life looks like. Of course, it differs for everyone depending on their specific passions and lives, but there are some general qualities of a passionate life.

It looks like this:

- You have a general sense of enthusiasm and purpose.
- You feel deeply engaged in your passionate pursuit.

- That engagement and the joy it brings spills over into other areas of your life.
- You are forced to simplify your life because you want to spend more time doing what you love.
- Problems and life difficulties diminish because you are happier and have fewer complications.
- You have better relationships because you are more attractive, positive, and interesting.
- You frequently experience the sense of being "in the flow."
- Even when you aren't proficient at your passion pursuit, you enjoy the practice of it and the process of learning.

Think about people you know who are living passionate lives. If you can't think of anyone, take a look at Oprah Winfrey, John Maxwell, or Tony Robbins. Is it worth pursuing a life passion? Only if you want a passionate life — like these people.

But so many people never find their life passion because they sabotage their search before they really get started. Here are some of the most common ways people undermine the most important pursuit they could ever undertake.

1. They don't believe it's possible. Sometimes people begin the process with serious doubts about finding their passion. They just fundamentally believe that life is meant to be difficult and that happiness and fulfillment are out of their control. Or they

believe the myths about finding their passion they may have heard or read.

2. They think life passion is silly, unrealistic, or too idealistic. There are those who believe the entire notion of having a life passion is indulgent at best and a waste of time at worst. Some people are not comfortable creating their life around happiness and purpose. Perhaps they are motivated by money, power, a sense of responsibility, or a general seriousness about life.

3. They don't give themselves the time. The journey of finding your life passion takes some time. It involves self-discovery work, research, trial and error, and experimentation. This requires carving an hour or two out of your week to work on it. But many people aren't proactive about this. They just hope that a life passion will magically appear.

4. They are overwhelmed. Their lives are so complicated, busy, cluttered, and over-scheduled that the idea of adding one more thing — even if it could create balance, order, and happiness — is too overwhelming. They put a passion search at the bottom of the priority list.

5. They aren't emotionally healthy. People who are living with depression, anxiety, anger, and other debilitating emotions don't have the energy to devote to finding their passion. They might try, but they will quickly lose enthusiasm and interest. The emotions need to be treated, and the root cause addressed, before beginning a passion search.

6. They are stuck in their thoughts. Thought without action will get you nowhere. Think through your options and the pros and cons. But eventually take action. People who are stuck in their thoughts are too afraid to do anything for fear it's the wrong decision. But a wrong decision is better than no decision, and often the wrong decision leads to something better than expected.

7. They underestimate themselves. Some people just don't believe they are capable of doing what needs to be done to create their lives around passion. They don't believe they're smart enough, creative enough, deserving enough or good enough. They assume that their perceived limitations will get in the way of living their passion even if they find it.

8. They give up too quickly. Finding a life passion involves trial and error, practice, and patience. Many people view the process of finding a passion to be confusing and arduous so they give up when the going gets hard. But it doesn't have to be hard. If you view the process the way you would perceive an interesting mystery, it can be fun and engaging. Most of the learning and growth happens in the process of the search.

Passion moves us out from our comfort zone. John Maxwell said, "To succeed in life, we must stay within our strength zone, but continually move outside our comfort zone."

It is hard for many to move outside their comfort zone. Most like to feel safe and secure putting them in a self-satisfying or comfortable position. However, this position kills passion. Picture the wings of a bird that have been clipped to keep it from soaring. That's what happens when we become self-satisfying or comfortable. It puts our hopes, dreams and desires beyond our reach.

In order to achieve our hopes, dreams, desires and our journey, take on the initiative to be successful. Be willing to take risks. Passion pushes you to take those risks. It prompts you to leave your comfort zone and cross the gateway to your success, away from doubt. It pushes us out the door and, on the way, to completing our journey.

The majority of people in the world don't follow their passion. Most are frustrated and unhappy. Their unhappiness is displayed in their everyday life. They just exist during the week and try to live it up on the weekends. What a sad state to be in.

In this 24/7, always moving world we live in today, there is a new hunger for meaning - for discovering how we matter. Purpose is the antidote to the busyness and emptiness for so many people's lives today.

Discovering your purpose is a lifelong process. You need passion to discover your purpose. During times of transition, we experience the greatest need and the greatest opportunity to create clarity of purpose for our lives. We reach higher and go deeper to discover what really matters.

There is a formula that can assist you in finding your purpose.
$$G + P + V = \text{Purpose}$$

You find your purpose when you offer your gifts in service to something you are passionate about in an environment that is consistent with your core values.

Sounds easy right? Well, it isn't rocket science, but will take some work. First, you want to identify your gifts, ask yourself:

- What do you do best? Our gifts are reflected in what we do best.
- Do you like to serve others? Our gifts show up in how we like to serve.
- How do you act when performing tasks? Our gifts are being used when we lose our self in a task.

Let's talk about passion. What's yours? If you are unsure, ask yourself these questions:

- If the pay didn't matter, what would I most love to do with my time?
- What problem at work or in my community would I love to solve?

Once you identify your gifts and your passion, we need to determine our values. To name your values, ask yourself these questions:

- If I reviewed how I spend my time and money, what would that tell me about what I most value?
- What are one or two life triggering events that have influenced what I value most?
- How do I want people to treat me?
- What is the best way to let someone know how I feel?
- How do I feel about my personal space?
- How do I feel about others personal space?
- How do I feel about the things I own?

There are many other questions you could ask yourself on values, but the answers to these questions will give you your best response.

So, how passionate are you about your journey? Do you wake up in the morning and go to sleep at night thinking about it? Does your passion feel like a fire pit burning inside of you? Are you willing to sacrifice other important things for it? Is the excitement of your journey so hot that it sets other people on fire? That's passion!

NOTES

Tenacity

Determined, persistent, tenacious, perseverance, stick-to-itiveness — whatever label you apply it's about hanging on through the challenges and bumps in the road to eventually achieve your goals.

Now, not to put too fine a point on it, but while each of these words represents the same fundamental ideology, I will admit to having a strong affinity for the concept of tenacity. It seems to me that tenacity is about so much more than not giving up on a goal. It's about focusing on growth, innovation and stretching ourselves beyond our normal boundaries.

"Persistence is doing something again and again until it works. Tenacity is using new data to make new decisions to find new pathways to find new ways to achieve goals when the old ways didn't work." ~Seth Godin

Standard goal setting advice subscribes to the importance of being realistic, and there's a lot to be said for that approach when it comes to many areas of life. But I also believe that when we focus solely on achieving what is 'realistic,' it's far too tempting to remain well within our current comfort zone. Where we achieve the most meaningful growth is when we challenge ourselves to go beyond what is comfortable, beyond what even seemed possible when we began the journey.

So, what does tenacity look like?

Tenacious people are planners, and while they are disciplined and apply an unwavering approach to going after their desired outcome, they clearly understand the difference between not giving up and stubbornly doing the same thing over and over hoping for a different outcome. I've seen stubbornness referred to as tenacity's ugly twin and I think that sums it up pretty well.

Those who are tenacious focus on growth with purpose so they continually evaluate their actions and progress; remain flexible and adjust their methods, and leave nothing to chance. They are masters at self-motivation, avid learners and have no qualms about asking for help when the need arises.

"The most difficult thing is the decision to act, the rest is merely tenacity. The fears are paper tigers. You can do anything you decide to do. You can act to change and control your life; and the procedure, the process is its own reward." ~Robyn Davidson

Let me stress before we go further that those who are tenacious learn early on the importance of mastering internal motivation. You see the initial excitement of setting a big, audacious goal is pretty heady stuff so it's understandable that you might want to share your exciting plans and enthusiasm. If you're fortunate enough to have forward thinking people in your support network, that's great ... however many find themselves faced with naysayers warning of the foolishness of attempting to achieve something so far beyond their current abilities or resources.

I admire people with tenacity. Have you ever seen someone so determined to get something done that their determination shows in everything they do? That's tenacity. They want to persevere no matter what their circumstances. They don't take "no" for an answer and they never give up. We see that in toddlers when trying to walk for the first time. Just because they fall, they don't give up. They keep going – they keep trying to walk.

Others qualities of people with tenacity are:

- Take another step even when they think they can't.
- Keep plugging away.
- Make small progress every day.
- They have staying power.
- They exhibit endurance and stamina.

Do you have the tenacity to go to the max to get what you want? Or when things get tough – and they will – are you likely to give up?

The difference between those who "see" their journey and those who "seize" their journey for success is tenacity.

Everyone faces difficulty. When someone fails, he makes excuses for what went wrong; how the unexpected happened; how someone interfered or how circumstances worked against him. Things don't stop you; you stop you. Tough to hear – I know.

Accept that adversity (or setbacks) will happen. They are a normal part of life. Good and bad things happen to us every day. It's how we respond to these "things" that matter. We need to accept responsibility for our share of the adversity. If you are able to acknowledge your share of responsibility, you will be better able to control the outcome. Give yourself permission to feel negative emotions, but set a time limit on how long you will allow them to continue. It's expected that adversity will cause us to feel bad. However, it is important to not allow setbacks to control our emotions.

When things go wrong, when the obstacles seem too great, when the difficulties get to be too much, when your journey seems to be impossibly far away, your job is to simply keep going.

Why do people fail to act on something they say is so important to them? What steps can you do to improve your tenacity, especially to overcome adversity?

- Don't wait for everything to be right to move forward – that's wrong.
- Watch what you say – change your vocabulary. Be willing to change your words from can't to can do.
- Think out of the box. Think of other ways to do things. Don't stick with the same ways of doing things. What

may have worked in the past will not work today. You can never exhaust all possibilities.

- Keep up your momentum. The minute your momentum stops, so do you and your resources.
- Change your perspective.
- Change your habits. If your habits and your journey don't match, then change your habits or change your journey.
- Spend time in nature. Numerous studies point to the healing impact of nature, as well as its impact on reducing stress and creating positive feelings. In turn, these positive feelings will outweigh the negative effects of the adversity.
- Develop characteristics such as: faith, courage, fortitude and resilience. The more of these qualities you have, the lesser the impact of the adversity. Building strong character allows us to develop better responses to deal with adversity.
- Believe in yourself. Understand that the setbacks happen, but that you have the power to overcome them.
- Focus on the future. "This too shall pass" is something we have all heard, and probably recited to others, on numerous occasions – because it's true. Adversity comes and goes, but it doesn't have to define us.

How we respond to adversity, setbacks, pain and problems, in both our thoughts and actions, is what makes us more successful and stronger individuals. Make adversity a learning opportunity to keep your tenacity in check. Address the setbacks, don't wallow in its difficulty and step forward to a better today and a brighter tomorrow.

Here are 10 steps to increase your tenacity:

1. Make Lists: What you love about yourself, who do you love to spend time with & what brings you passion and joy? Once it is all written down - breathe - and be that person you just wrote about.

2. Ignore the Naysayers. This is an important factor in being true to yourself. If there is a ripple effect of negativity as you make positive changes, this is ok. I know it is uncomfortable but being YOU is much savvier than creating an image so others are satisfied.

3. Align Your Heart with Your Steps. Which direction are your feet walking? Are they walking towards what you are passionate about in your heart?

4. Accept Yourself. Figure out who are you and when you do, accept yourself with unconditional loving arms. Don't waste another second comparing yourself to others or concerning yourself with what others think. It truly does not matter unless you want it to. You get to decide.

5. Let Go. Let go of the past, it's over. Let go of other's expectations. Let go of your worry for the future. Just be. Simply

being in the moment and showing up as your true self is beyond romantic, lovely, sexy, brave and honorable.

6. Review your goals. Do you have a compelling vision for each goal? Just saying you want something will not be enough once life starts to get in the way. It's crucial for you to flesh out the details of each goal, so you can really see them in your mind. It's a precursor to manifesting them.

7. Maintain motivation. As individuals, we are motivated by both reward and pain. I find that it's helpful to visualize, in great detail, what benefits will come to you by achieving your goals and what consequences will be yours if you don't.

8. Set your intention. Take a few minutes before you go to bed each night to identify one thing that you can do to move forward with one of your goals. Keep it small and simple. They will add up.

9. Ask for support. Identify the areas you need improvement and ask others for help. Your friends and family want you to succeed. And many of them might also want to feel needed by you. So, asking for help allows you to get some needed strength and perhaps even build your relationship at the same time.

10. Give yourself credit. Often times, people give up because they don't get where they want to be fast enough. Along the way, discouragement and self-doubt kick in and people throw in the towel. Take time each day to recall the positive things you

did to move forward in your life, whether big or small. The more you focus on what you've done, the more you will stay engaged in the journey.

My point in sharing this with you is that above all those who are tenacious are passionate about achieving their dreams so they are not easily distracted or discouraged.

The bottom line ...Let's be honest, this notion of going for BIG unrealistic dreams is not for everyone and that's okay. But for those who dare, it's also important to bear in mind that such adventures are rarely undertaken in a vacuum. We begin by going for a goal that is just a little out of reach, something that requires we obtain new knowledge and learn new skills in order to achieve, and then continue to build on each successful accomplishment.

This is an approach that can be mastered by any determined individual, and it is surprisingly easy to know if and when you're ready to make the leap, because it inevitably boils down to just how badly you want to achieve something, to be uncommon.

How about you? Do you tenaciously pursue your dreams and goals? Have you set BIG goals that require you to reach beyond your comfort zone?

Let today be the day you give up who you've been for who you can become.

Tenacity

NOTES

Wisdom

Wisdom can be gathered.
Wisdom can be learned or gained.
Wisdom cannot be taught.

Knowledge, Wisdom, and Insight may sound like synonyms, but they are not. Though they all refer to the mind and an accumulation of thoughts and experiences, they have some very real differences in the essence of their meanings and their applications in our life.

Knowledge is the accumulation of facts and data that you have learned about or experienced. It's being aware of something, and having information. Knowledge is really about facts and ideas that we acquire through study, research, investigation, observation, or experience.

Wisdom is the ability to discern and judge which aspects of that knowledge are true, right, lasting, and applicable to your life. It's the ability to apply that knowledge to the greater scheme of life. It's also deeper; knowing the meaning or reason; about knowing why something is, and what it means to your life.

Insight is the deepest level of knowing and the most meaningful to your life. Insight is a deeper and clearer perception of life, of knowledge, of wisdom. It's grasping the underlying nature of knowledge, and the essence of wisdom. Insight is a truer understanding of your life and the bigger picture of how things intertwine.

In a nutshell: If knowledge is information, wisdom is the understanding and application of that knowledge and insight is the awareness of the underlying essence of a truth.

Sadly, we can gain a lifetime of knowledge, yet never see the wisdom in it. We can be wise, but still miss the deeper meaning.

This may help sum up the differences:

- Knowledge is knowing how to manage your money, budgeting, spending, and saving.

- Wisdom is understanding how money impacts the quality of your life and your future.

- Insight is realizing that money is simply a tool to be used, that it has no inherent meaning beyond its usefulness.

- Knowledge is knowing which things, practices, people, and pleasures make you happy.

- Wisdom is knowing that while those things may bring you pleasure, happiness is not derived from things or situations or people. It's understanding that happiness comes from within, and that it's a temporary state of mind.

- Insight is knowing that happiness is not the purpose of life, that it's not the marker of the quality of life—it's merely one of the many fleeting states of mind in the spectrum of full emotions. Those emotions don't make up our lives; they are merely experiences.

Knowledge, wisdom and insight all are valuable and all have a place in our lives. The difficulty lies in the fact that many of us are unclear as to their differences, often perceiving the terms and their application to be interchangeable. Being clear and consciously aware of how our minds are engaged may be important to getting the most out of all three. While acquiring and applying information is valuable in and of itself, we also need to distill and judge that information, and ultimately find the deeper meaning and relevance to the whole of our lives. Perhaps the truest form of knowing is in acquiring all three, and understanding how they each enhance the quality and experience of life.

Wisdom is what beckons us to speak. Wisdom always raises others with images of a better way. Women are endowed with both intuition and insight, which give us the awareness of something on a perceptive, intuitive level without actual evidence of its existence – a glimpse into the realm of the unseen and possible. Wise women are a gift to their culture. When a woman fosters beauty in and through her life and home, practices discretion, heeds godly instructions, and bestows wisdom, there is no greater source of inspiration.

So, is Faith the "Magical Ingredient for Wisdom?"

A lot of individuals believe in God. They presume He exists, but He is not tangible enough to them to affect what they think and accomplish.

To believe in God, on the other hand, is to have faith that God will do for us whatsoever He has promised to accomplish. He expects us to act on that trust. He demands that we have living faith in His existence, mightiness and promises. Faith isn't some magic ingredient. Faith leads to a confident attitude towards The Higher Power. Faith incites our minds to the assurance of God's mightiness and will to act in our lives.

Faith gets to be more than a mental conviction as it develops into a commitment, not simply to trust God to get involved in our lives, but to do His will.

Faith is belief. But let's not arrive at the age-old error of believing that if we believe in God—that is, that He lives—we therefore have faith. A lot of people hold to this misguided idea. They say they believe in God; they think, therefore, they have faith.

To believe in God is simply our beginning point of faith. A spiritual realm lies all about us, enveloping us, embracing us, altogether inside reach of our internal selves, waiting for us to recognize it. God Himself is here awaiting our reaction to His presence. God and the spiritual world are real. We might believe that with as much confidence as we believe the familiar world around us.

Spiritual things are here inviting our attention and challenging our trust. Faith isn't wishful thinking, a pie-in-the-sky feeling that everything will be perfect. Faith is a deep strong belief that God deeply cares for us and will constantly act with our best interests at heart.

Every one of us needs this sort of faith. We need it if we wish to honor and love God, as "But without faith it is impossible to please Him: for he that comes to God must believe that He is, and that He is a rewarder of them that diligently seek Him." Hebrews 11:6

Altering our lives to submit to God—what the Bible refers to as repentance—is based on the strong belief that He will intervene in our lives and in the final analysis grant us eternal life.

Merely saying "I believe" without arriving at accompanying life-altering changes isn't sufficient. The faith required for salvation includes not only comprehending what God desires from us, but in addition to that our acting on that understanding.

When you think about wisdom, wisdom is a pretty broad spectrum. Many people associate education with wisdom, although there isn't a huge difference between the two, we can define education as a formal process received from a college, university or other type of school, and wisdom is an informal process which is gained through real-life experience.

The distinguishing factor is whether you are paying to go to school versus wisdom that you gain from personal life experience. Wisdom is not an automatic process. It's something to seek out and acquire from our own self-effort. Our brain is wired to acquire new information until the day we die. God commands us to seek wisdom and understanding. There is a proverb that states "Seek knowledge and whatever price you must pay for it, pay for it." We aren't just talking about wisdom that we get from real-life experiences, but wisdom that we seek out.

Usually the wisdom that comes to us through our experiences may not always be pleasant. If we want to seek out better experiences, how does one acquire the wisdom they need - especially if they don't know what they need? In some circumstances we don't know what we don't know. You can be in a bad situation and think that is the way it is supposed to be. Many people think it is the cards that were dealt to them. If you have a voice inside of you saying something isn't right, that is your subconscious telling you there is a better life out there for you. Learning is difficult. Learning is work. You have to make the effort to go out and obtain the wisdom to get you out of these bad situations.

If we think back on our elementary school days, we know learning isn't easy. But what steps can you take to get seek wisdom?

- Seek help in your local church.
- Talk to your Pastor. They can also direct to someone that can help you.
- Speak to a Counselor.
- Seek out a Personal Life Coach.
- Find a Therapist
- Visit your local library or book store and look at books on a self-help shelf to see what is offered.

We have to be humble and vulnerable enough to say "I don't know" and want to find someone that does know and can help us. We have to be proactive. The strength of our efforts is the measure of our results. The more effort you put into something, the more you will get out of it. If you keep performing the same actions, you will get the same results. This is so much for women to realize. But it is so worth the effort to make their life better, not just for themselves but for the next generation. When a woman is kept down, her kids may be kept down. I want women to step up and realize they deserve better and their kids deserve better. If we are in a place we don't want our children and grand-children to be, take the steps to lift ourselves out of that position. The generations to come will reap the rewards.

In order to seek wisdom, one must have confidence. Self-confidence can be nothing more than knowing exactly the extent of what our capabilities are. Learning how to acquire knowledge about your own skills and all the positive traits you have will help you to be more self-confident. An exercise that will help you is to take a piece of paper and write down your strengths on one side and your areas of improvement (or as others refer to it - weaknesses) on the other. As you read over the list of strengths, your self-confidence will increase. You may not realize how many skills you have until you read them for yourself. I love this exercise. I've done it many times. When I reviewed my strengths, I could easily volunteer in areas where I was well-suited. It really opens your eyes to what you are capable of.

On the other side of the paper where your areas of improvement are, that is where you will focus on the knowledge for those areas. Where we are weak, God is strong. By writing these down we can pray to God for the areas we need improvement – especially the areas of blind spots - so we can put our best foot forward to where God needs us.

What are some of the road blocks that keep women from gathering the knowledge or wisdom they need? It's the road block of self-doubt that someone has instilled in you. Things like:

- When you are told over and over "you are no good" you eventually believe "you are no good."
- Lack of access to a proper education.
- Finances are a road block (which is unfortunate.)

You can acquire knowledge and education by talking to older people and those with more experience. The elders in a church are a great reference. Did you know - the most precious gift you can give someone is your time?

A recent article I read stated some of the top billionaires don't have a college education. I want you to realize it's not a matter of education. If God places something on your heart, if you take the steps to seek out that knowledge, he is going to make it happen. Another article worth mentioning was about dreams. It states that when our dreams are so vivid it is because in God's perspective they have already occurred, because he knows things from beginning to end. He knows the dream – even though they seem far off to us, in his calendar they are already complete. Walk toward them and look to take all this in. We serve an abundant God and of the roadblocks you listed, there is nothing he cannot provide for us. Matthew 7:7 says "Ask, and it shall be given you; seek, and ye shall find; knock, and it shall be opened unto you".

Know and listen to the voice inside of you saying there is a better life for you and tell yourself "I'm going to find it!" Ask in your heart for God to show you YOUR better life.

Every day, whether we interact with 5 people, 50 people, or 500, our lives matter and produce a ripple effect that extends far beyond us. Let's model authenticity, celebrate beauty, have clarity, have faith, be a great influence, live our passion, celebrate growth, encourage strength, and obtain the wisdom we need for a great life.

Be proud of yourself and your accomplishments. Take Action today!

NOTES

Conclusion

I know how it feels when the universe is working against you, believe me. When everyone is telling you to do the opposite of what you want, telling you to move on, telling you to wait, telling you it isn't worth it. It is worth it.

At some point in our lives, we find a few things we hold so tightly we think we can never let them go. We find that boy and give him our heart. We find that dream destination miles away and set our minds on living there. At some point, we wake up and we know what's important and what isn't; we know what we want and what we don't.

Give yourself permission to want something so desperately you can actually feel your heart aching for it. Seems like more often than not people are numb, content with mediocrity, chasing only what is easy and that isn't how it should be.

Fight for it. If you wake up thinking about it, and by the time you lay down to sleep the thoughts haven't stopped but only intensified, then please fight for it. There's a reason you can't let go, a reason you can't accept the tiny town forever, can't accept defeat without giving 110% first, but it's not because you're stubborn. It's because you have something special.

You have the ability, the intuition, and wisdom - all that you need to see the absolute best in everything, and everyone. You've spent your life determining what situations deserve your time and efforts and which ones don't. You know which people are worth your time and which ones you should move on from. You've spent your life protecting yourself and being cautious. When you come to a crossroad in your life, and you can't decide what to do, choose the path which will make you the happiest, not the people around you. This is your life and you're the one who has to live it.

You can't force people to see what you have to offer; you can't force people to care the same way that you do; you can't force people to understand your vision; but in the end, if you've given it your all, you have nothing to be ashamed of. Remain a good person, a strong, selfless, pure person. Be the absolute best version of yourself, even when things seem out of reach or out of control. That is the version which will take you places in life.

You must know that you can survive without these things, without the boy, without the house on the beach, but if you want them, don't give up. These are your dreams, things that are important to you and I've always been told if you want something you have to work for it. Nothing in this life comes easy, so yes lady, if you want it, you have to fight for it.

Take that first step today. Take action today!

Conclusion

NOTES

NOTES

Conclusion

NOTES

Index

Take Action, 5, 24, 25, 52, 75, 78
Tenacious, 57, 58, 64
Tenacity, 57-62
Tony Robbins, 50
Trust, 6, 11, 43, 70, 71

W
Wisdom, 67-75, 77

About the Author

MICHELE SFAKIANOS (Sfa-can-iss) is a Registered Nurse, Leading Authority on Parenting and Life Skills, Speaker, Certified Personal Coach and an Award-winning Author. Her books and programs provide the answers you've always wanted to many of life's difficult "who/what/why/where/when and how-to" questions. Her experience as a Registered Nurse, mother and grandmother, along with her extensive training qualifies her as an expert in her field. Michele has two college degrees (Nursing and Computer Programming) and several certifications (Personal Coaching, Legal Nursing, Copywriting and Real Estate).

She has won many awards for her books including: 2012 Indie Excellence Winner; 2012 Gold Medal Living Now Book Awards; 2013 Bronze Medal Readers' Favorite Book Award; 2013 Gold Medal Wise Bear Digital Book Awards; and multiple Honorable Mentions. Michele has the desire to help others reach their full potential by providing information in a concise, direct-to-the-point, manner. She knows your time is valuable and strives to provide you the information you need, quickly and accurately, to unlock your potential. Let Michele help you to be the success you were meant to be!

Open Pages Publishing is a self-publishing company offering books to inspire, teach, and inform readers. We specialize in a variety of subjects including: life skills, self-help, reference, parenting, leadership and teens.

Ordering Information:

Open Pages Publishing books are available at major online bookstores. They may also be purchased for educational, business, or promotional use.

For bulk orders: special discounts are available on bulk orders. For details contact our sales staff at info@openpagespublishing.com.

Visit openpagespublishing.com for a list of books by Michele Sfakianos

ENJOY THE READ

Open Pages Publishing, LLC is happy to be able to share this information with you. We sincerely hope you will share your selection with others. The simplest way to do that is to review/rate it for us on Amazon, the world's largest bookseller in the world.

If you have time, and if you enjoyed the book, please consider rating it for us; We humbly thank you.

Open Pages Publishing, LLC

NOTES

NOTES

www.ingramcontent.com/pod-product-compliance
Lightning Source LLC
La Vergne TN
LVHW051424080426
835508LV00022B/3233